MAD LOVE

Marisa Smith

BROADWAY PLAY PUBLISHING INC
New York
www.broadwayplaypublishing.com
info@broadwayplaypublishing.com

MAD LOVE premiered at Northern Stage in Vermont running from 17 January13 -February 2016. The cast and creative contributors were:

BRANDON .... Thom Miller
SLOANe ....Alex Trow
DOUG .... Daniel Patrick Smith
KATERINA ....Laurel Castillo

Director .... Maggie Burrows
Set Designer ....David L. Arsenault
Costume Designer ....Allison Crutchfield
Lighting Designer .... Greg Solomon
Music design .... Theo Speilberg
Music .... Wardell
Production Stage Manager .... Jess Johnston

MAD LOVE was subsquently produced at New Jersey Repertory Company running from 20 October-20 November 2016. The cast and creative contributors were:

BRANDON .... Graham Techler
SLOANE .... Alex Trow
DOUG .... Jared Delaney
KATERINA .... Brittany Proia

Director .... Evan Bergman
Set Designer .... Jessica Parks
Costume design .... Patricia E. Doherty
Lighting design .... Jill Nagle
Sound design .... Merek Royce Press
Production Stage Manager .... Jennifer Tardibuono
Technical Director .... Brian Synder

CHARACTERS & SETTING

SLOANE, 26, *smart, sharp, beautiful, had a privileged upbringing on the Upper East Side of New York City, scarred by the hookup culture of modern life but very adept at covering deep wells of emotion.*

BRANDON, *20s, responsible, loyal, a stand-up guy, wise, an old soul.*

DOUG, BRANDON's *older brother, late 20s to late 30s, open, eternal adolescent, warm, emotionally accessible, a shaggy dog. A survivor.*

KATERINA, *in her late 20s, originally from Estonia, savvy, sexy, confident, speaks with an Eastern European accent.*

Note on the set: There are four locations in the play: the restaurant, the men's apartment, BRANDON's *classroom and the boardwalk and beach at Coney Island. The set can be non-realistic with just suggestions of the particular location.*

Scene One

(An upscale restaurant in New York City.)

(BRANDON and SLOANE walk to their table.)

SLOANE: And don't worry, this is my treat, I invited *you.*

BRANDON: *(Hesitantly)* Well, we could split it…

SLOANE: Absolutely not, it's my deal.

BRANDON: But—

SLOANE: I should pay, I called this meeting.

BRANDON: Meeting? This is a meeting?

(BRANDON and SLOANE sit and pick up their menus.)

SLOANE: Yeah, my Dad's coming.

(BRANDON looks around, nervous.)

SLOANE: *(Laughing)* Just kidding. This is fun, we've never gone out to dinner—or out period, haha.

BRANDON: Sloane, this is a little bizarre—what are we doing here?

SLOANE: *(Ignoring him)* You look nice. I've never seen you with a jacket on…or fully clothed, come to think of it.

BRANDON: You said it was fancy. Seriously, what gives?

SLOANE: Patience, young jedi, patience. Relax, can you do that?

(SLOANE *puts her hands lightly on* BRANDON*'s shoulders and pushes them down.*)

(BRANDON *takes a deep breath and drops his shoulders.*)

BRANDON: Fine.

SLOANE: Good. So how's school, how are the little monsters?

BRANDON: I told this girl she was *sassy* and she complained to the Principal.

SLOANE: Are you kidding? Sassy? What's wrong with sassy?

BRANDON: Beats me, it's sexist or something.

SLOANE: She just wants attention. She's probably crushing on you, Mr Fitz. (*Back to her menu*) Do *I* want Duck with Five Lilies and Kumquat Vinaigrette or do I want Branzino with Lemon Oregano Jam?

BRANDON: (*Does a Jimmy Stewart/George Bailey impression*) You want the Duck, Mary? Just say the word and I'll throw a lasso around it and pull it down.

SLOANE: (*Laughing*) Et tu, George Baily, what'll you have?

BRANDON: Diver scallops with Babbo Pancetta— whatever that is.

SLOANE: Pancetta is Italian bacon and Babbo means Dad. Daddy bacon I guess.

BRANDON: Of course you know.

SLOANE: Oh stop, I'm sure there lots of things you know that I don't. Like what a…wing-nut *really* is, or what…*prevent defense* means. See?

BRANDON: You are so weird. You are so so weird.

SLOANE: (*Reaching for cocktail menu*) And I'm gonna have a super fun cocktail. Something I've never had before. (*Studying the menu*) "Purple Haze!!" Ohmygod it changes color, from blue to purple while you drink it! *"Purple Haze!"* I have to have that! Don't you?

BRANDON: I was actually thinking whatever's on draft.

SLOANE: You want one, c'mon. It changes color! It's *celebratory* and I have a very special announcement!

BRANDON: Is that why we're here?

SLOANE: Sort of. I've been promoted!

BRANDON: Congratulations.

SLOANE: And don't you wanna know *why?*

BRANDON: Because your Dad owns the company?

SLOANE: Because I came up with the name of the new fragrance for our celebrity client whose name I cannot say— *(She sings.)* "Like a Vir-gin…

(BRANDON joins SLOANE singing.)

BRANDON & SLOANE: …for the very first time…"

BRANDON: *(Pretending)* I have no idea who that is.

SLOANE: It's so perfect, unbelievably perfect for her. But you can't tell anyone. It's top secret.

BRANDON: Fine, I promise.

SLOANE: Okay. It's…*Tumescence.*

BRANDON: What?

SLOANE: Tumescence.

BRANDON: O-kay. Tumescence.

SLOANE: *(Whispers very dramatically)* Tumescence.

BRANDON: Okay. It sounds good. Perfumy.

SLOANE: You have no idea what it means, do you?

BRANDON: Not really. But I feel it like it has something to do with…

SLOANE: With what?

BRANDON: With sex.

SLOANE: You're right! Exactly! It sounds *sexy*, right?

BRANDON: Yeah. But what *does* it mean?

SLOANE: …Engorged, it means engorged, swollen. But tumescence is so much better, don't you think?

BRANDON: Yuh, yuh, much better.

SLOANE: And that horrible Alison's not my boss anymore. Make your own smoothies bitch.

BRANDON: Right, the one with the cheeseburger in her drawer?

SLOANE: Now she's always slamming this frozen bag of peas on her neck.

BRANDON: Gross.

SLOANE: The day I have my first hot flash is the day I'm going to kill myself.

BRANDON: Sloane.

SLOANE: She never had any kids, which I think is so sad, don't you think that's sad?

BRANDON: Maybe she didn't want any.

SLOANE: I think it's *tragic* when a woman exits this universe without having popped one out. That's what we're here for when you get right down to it.

BRANDON: Is that like post-feminism feminism?

SLOANE: No, it's the truth, it's the bottom line! I mean, what's the point if you don't procreate? Tell me, why are we here, why?

BRANDON: To have a really, really good time?

SLOANE: Wrong. I mean I hate babies—

BRANDON: You *hate* babies.

SLOANE: But I'm sure I'd like them if they were mine.

BRANDON: Nice to know you wouldn't *eat* them.

SLOANE: Brandon, you are going to *love* this. I got you this great gig.

BRANDON: *(Wary)* Gig? What gig?

SLOANE: So one of our clients, Yip Yardley? —designed these prom dresses?

BRANDON: Yip? Yup.

SLOANE: And we're having a fashion show this Friday and we're short one guy and I realized you'd be *perfect* because we need like a *regular* ol' guy, I mean…a *real* person and you totally fit the bill! Plus you can keep the tux.

(BRANDON *says nothing.*)

SLOANE: You can KEEP the tux.

BRANDON: Okay.

SLOANE: Great, I'll drop it off at your apartment tomorrow, how's that?

BRANDON: No, that's okay, I can pick it up.

SLOANE: How come you don't ever want me to come to your apartment? Are you married or something?

BRANDON: *(Holds up his left hand)* Twenty-five beautiful years. No!! No, it's just a mess.

SLOANE: Oh fine, just text me your address. I'll have someone from the office leave it with the doorman?

BRANDON: The *super*, Sloane. Carlos. First floor.

SLOANE: Thanks. And…

BRANDON: And what?

SLOANE: I have this other…issue.

BRANDON: Okay. Go ahead.

(Pause)

SLOANE: Would you consider being my sperm donor?

(*Beat*)

BRANDON: Your...*sperm* donor?

SLOANE: You're familiar with the term.

BRANDON: Are you kidding?

SLOANE: Look, here's the deal. I'm twenty-six years old. Statistically fertility for women begins to drop at age *twenty-seven* so I want to have a baby before I'm thirty. Also, my body will bounce back then. I mean I still want to wear a bikini after kids.

BRANDON: You're not serious.

SLOANE: Of course I'm serious, I've gotta get moving! Time flies Brandon. Every day we die. Die a little death. Die. Die. Die.

BRANDON: You're *young*.

SLOANE: Not young biologically.

BRANDON: You're jumping the gun, aren't you? I mean, someday—you'll get married, Sloane—

SLOANE: C'mon, it's *obvious* I'll never get married, I'm not the marrying kind! We're allergic to marriage in our family. My mother did it four times and didn't get it right and my Dad? His new wife, are you ready?-- is only *four years* older than I am. We could have been in college together-—

BRANDON: That doesn't matter, it's not a genetic thing Sloane—

SLOANE: Forget about it! Also, I get tired of people, with guys. I mean no offense, I'm not tired of you yet-- but I know WHO I AM! I am not gonna get married.

BRANDON: So what...I can't even believe I'm asking this...you want me to get you pregnant?

SLOANE: No! I'd *buy* it. I'd pay for your sperm and I'd freeze it. And use it when I wanted.

BRANDON: You'd *pay* me?

SLOANE: Of course I'd pay you.

BRANDON: You'd pay me for my sperm.

SLOANE: Yes. *(Pause)* Like, serious drachmas. That was what the Greeks used before—

BRANDON: I know what drachmas are Sloane!

SLOANE: Yes, well, like a lot of them.

BRANDON: That's crazy, you could go to a sperm bank for practically nothing-—

SLOANE: I don't want some *stranger's* DNA. I wanna know what I'm getting! I mean you're really smart and frankly, the blue-collar roots work in your favor. You know—good genes, hardy, strong. No allergies?

BRANDON: Strawberries.

SLOANE: *(Thinking)* You'll outgrow it. *(Recovering)* And you'd have no legal responsibility whatsoever. I'd sign something. My lawyer would do lunch with your lawyer.

BRANDON: Sloane, forget it, I'd never do it.

SLOANE: Well, I just wanted to plant the seed, haha.

BRANDON: No way.

SLOANE: *(Frantically waving)* I see our waiter!! Yes! *"Purple Haze!"*

BRANDON: It's a totally crackpot idea.

SLOANE: Will you at least *consider* my offer?

BRANDON: No.

SLOANE: Bran-don.

BRANDON: No. No. *No.* NO.

(Blackout)

Scene Two

(Later that evening)

(Lights up on the living room/kitchen area of BRANDON *and* DOUG*'s apartment.)*

(It's messy, like a frat room. Pairs of women's panties are having on the wall.)

(There is a large recycling bin on the floor and a glass aquarium that houses Pogo, a pet Bearded Dragon.)

*(*BRANDON *enters carrying a grocery bag, and the mail. The door is open.)*

BRANDON: Doug? Doug? Are you here? Doug?

*(*DOUG *enters from an interior room; he's a large man a few years older than* BRANDON*, unkempt, wild looking, wears an old robe and flip-flops. He's eating a bowl of cereal.)*

DOUG: My man! Buffer! Was drainin' my monster, sorry.

BRANDON: Bro, the door was unlocked, that's bad, I've told you a million times—

DOUG: Hey, how are you?

BRANDON: You should *never* leave the door open man, are you okay? *(He goes to kitchen area to put away groceries.)*

DOUG: I'm great, I'm fanfuckingtastic.

BRANDON: Listen, I got a call from Mr Kim. He said you didn't show up for work again. What's up dude, you gotta go to work.

DOUG: It's this chick at work, she's creeping me out, I mean she's really coming on to me, she follows me around and kinda whispers. I don't know what the fuck she's saying.

BRANDON: Just ignore her.

DOUG: I can't man, wherever I go, she's like there. I unload the fruit and she's like under the boxes, I stock the shelves and she's like under my armpit. She's a ghost, man, and it's freaking me out.

BRANDON: I'll say something to Mr Kim. You gotta go back, you gotta go back tomorrow. *(He goes to get a beer in the frig.)*

DOUG: Her name is Jin-Souk. Jin-Souk. Maybe I should ask her out.

(BRANDON *returns with a beer in one hand and the mail in the other.)*

BRANDON: NO! Don't do that, no. She's probably Kim's daughter or something, don't do that.

DOUG: Relax, I'm kidding. Shit, I don't even know if she's real.

BRANDON: *(Alarmed)* What? What do you mean?

DOUG: I'm just pulling your chain. God, you are so lame.

BRANDON: Are you doing those brain exercises? I don't see your computer. Where's the computer Doug?

DOUG: *(Looking at Pogo)* You get Pogo a mango? He's really into mangoes these days.

BRANDON: So where's the computer bro?

DOUG: Take the cork out of your asshole, asshole. It's right here. *(Fishes computer out from under his couch cushion.)*

BRANDON: What's it doing there? You could break it!

DOUG: It's protected! I can remember it's there.

BRANDON: You've got to keep it on a flat surface! Seriously, you could sit on it and… Listen, I can't afford to buy you another computer, Doug.

DOUG: I'm not gonna break it… *(He opens the computer.)* See, all's its little gigabytes are just jumping up and fucking down.

BRANDON: I'm serious Doug. You gotta do those brain exercises, they're good for you.

DOUG: *(Lying down on couch)* Okay, okay, whatevs. You get cookies? Chips Ahoy?

(BRANDON *makes a face like he forgot and then breaks into a smile and laughs.)*

BRANDON: Yeah, on the counter.

DOUG: I'm *so* comfortable. *(Looking at ceiling)* I wanna put stars on the ceiling that glow in the dark. *(He whines like a dog.)*

BRANDON: Doug! Douglas!

(BRANDON *hesitates but then weakens. He gets up to fetch the cookies. On his way he picks up the recycling bin.)*

BRANDON: It should be in the kitchen dude.

(DOUG *tosses his empty beer can from the coffee table into the bin as* BRANDON *passes by.)*

DOUG: Touchdown! C'mon man. Why does the recycling have to be in the kitchen when we drink our brewskis out here? Think a little "out of the box."

BRANDON: *(Opening the mail)* God I'm sick of people telling me to think "out of the box". I hate that expression, it's such a cliché and it's time for it to leave the lexicon.

DOUG: Leave the lexicon? Man you are weird. Sometimes I don't know whose brain is more fucked up, yours or mine.

BRANDON: Shit.

DOUG: What?

BRANDON: Just bill crap.

(BRANDON *closes his eyes.* DOUG *looks worried.*)

DOUG: Are we okay?

BRANDON: Yeah.

DOUG: You sure? Money-wise?

BRANDON: We're fine Doug.

DOUG: People like to help dude. The Bradley's helped us once, didn't they?

BRANDON: I'm not asking the Bradley's again.

DOUG: Dad gave us those baseball cards.

BRANDON: Do not start with the fucking baseball cards again.

DOUG: Or what about your boy Arthur, the pimp?

BRANDON: He's not a pimp! He's a stockbroker.

DOUG: But he gets girls.

BRANDON: Yeah, for parties. He's like in charge of *entertainment.*

DOUG: Dude, sometimes you surprise me.

BRANDON: Hey, if everybody's happy.

DOUG: Why don't you marry one of your girlfriends? Are any of 'em rich?

BRANDON: Get married?

DOUG: What about that math teacher, Shayna, who doesn't wear undies?

BRANDON: She is married. And she doesn't wear a *bra.* And she's definitely not rich.

DOUG: The chick with the loft, is she flush?

BRANDON: I dunno, maybe. Marci.

DOUG: Marci. So?

BRANDON: I can't talk to her, she doesn't get my jokes.

DOUG: Sorry man, but your jokes suck. What about the one who beats you in tennis?

BRANDON: Sloane? Oh God.

DOUG: Sloane, she sounds upper crusty.

BRANDON: Yeah, her Dad's Mr Venture Capital—*Lansing* Hudson, a total pinhead.

DOUG: There ya go!

BRANDON: No, Sloane's just slumming it with me, are you kidding? Just biding her time 'til Mister Megarich comes along.

DOUG: Buff, cut it out, chicks love you!

(BRANDON *chuckles to himself and starts to tell* DOUG *about* SLOANE *but then stops himself.*)

DOUG: What?

BRANDON: Nuthin'.

DOUG: What? Buff!

BRANDON: Jesus, you won't believe this. She, Sloane, asked me if I'd be her *sperm donor*.

DOUG: Dude! She wants your sperm?

(*Pause*)

BRANDON: She's nuts.

DOUG: Why does she want your sperm?

BRANDON: Because she doesn't think she'll ever get married and she wants a kid before she's thirty.

DOUG: Does she want mine?

BRANDON: She wants to *freeze* it and then use it when she's ready.

DOUG: Like she'd put it in the freezer with the ice cream and shit?

BRANDON: And she said she'd *pay* me for it.

DOUG: She'd pay you? How much is she gonna pay you?

BRANDON: I'm not doing it Doug. It's a stupid idea.

DOUG: C'mon, how much?

BRANDON: I dunno. She didn't say. *(Pause)* A lot.

DOUG: A lot? She said *a lot* and she's loaded? That means a *ton.*

BRANDON: It's not that simple.

DOUG: Give her your spermskis, pass go, and collect the cash!

BRANDON: I mean sometimes I think she's crazy, and I should bail anyway… Get this, get this. She hates babies—

DOUG: Then why's she want one?

BRANDON: —unless they're hers. This is the position. She brags about it. Who says things like that?

DOUG: That's *honest!* Would you like other people's barfing, pooping little rugrats?
Do it man, you *gotta* do it! Take the money on the table!

BRANDON: If she uses my—sperm—then we're bonded for life. You realize that.

DOUG: She probably won't. Take a shot! DO IT! Slooooane. Very fancy. All your women… *(Starts unzipping his pants)* Is your dick bigger than mine? Did we ever check? Like really check?

BRANDON: Jesus, Doug. We are not going to compare dicks. *(He rises.)* Listen, I'm going for a walk. And you gotta go back to work, I'm serious.

DOUG: You're going for a *smoke*, c'mon, you said you'd quit.

BRANDON: I'll quit when you go back to work.

DOUG: I will if you call Arthur and get me a chick for my birthday!

BRANDON: NO!

DOUG: C'mon. It's my special day!

BRANDON: *(Opening the door)* No. No. NO. No. *(He exits and slams the door.)*

(DOUG pulls his waistband open, takes a look and smiles.)

(Blackout)

Scene Three

(The next day)

(BRANDON's classroom. Portraits of US Presidents festoon the walls.)

(BRANDON is on his phone, pacing, holding a piece of paper in his hands.)

BRANDON: No, I'm her son, her *son*, I'm not her husband, the form should say *son*, God. No. No, I was told she was *grandfathered*, that the policy wouldn't change. No, that's not true, she *is* covered, I don't know why you got it back, maybe you put the numbers in wrong. *(Listening to the person on the other end and looking at his paper)* No, no, NO, it's three one four one, three ONE four ONE, not three FOUR FOUR one! You know like *Pi*, three one four one. What? No, not that kind of pie, no forget it, forget it, it's not important. It's a number in math, it doesn't matter. I'm sorry, I didn't mean anything, I'm sorry, Kristen. *Kirsten*, sorry. I'm sure you were good in math. Yeah, I mean you'd have to be good to do your job, definitely. Absolutely. So, great, you'll re-submit? That would be *fantastic*. Thank you so much! Sure, you too, have a great day Kristen! Sorry, *Kirsten, Kirsten. (Hangs up phone and yells)* Kristen, Kirsten. Whatever!

(SLOANE *enters and hears* BRANDON.)

SLOANE: Brandon?

BRANDON: Sloane!

SLOANE: So, this is Mr Fitz's homeroom? I hear he's a wicked hard grader but really cute! God, who were you yelling at on the phone?

BRANDON: Oh, nothing, just insurance bullshit. How'd you get through security?

SLOANE: I said I was your sister. Your *twin* sister.

BRANDON: My twin sister?

SLOANE: The twin part really threw them off. I'm not staying, I know you're busy. I couldn't resist seeing you in your native habitat. *(Looking around)* Love the Presidents.

BRANDON: It's just a classroom.

SLOANE: *(Flirtatiously)* No, it's very cool. You know I still don't really understand the electoral college thing.

BRANDON: Look, it's great to see you but—

SLOANE: I just wanted to thank you for doing the show. And Yip is just over the moon.

BRANDON: Terrific.

SLOANE: And, I wanted to know if you've had some time to think about my other idea—

BRANDON: Sloane, you don't need a sperm donor.

SLOANE: I am dead serious.

(Beat)

BRANDON: Look. Allow me to remind you. People fall in love and get married and have babies every second, and that will ultimately be your fate. You don't need to be out there—buying sperm.

SLOANE: I'm not gonna fall in love. It's not in my genetic code, Brandon. My Dad said I have a very narrow emotional spectrum and he's right, I do.

BRANDON: A what? A very narrow emotional spectrum? What is that? I don't even know what that *is*!

SLOANE: And besides, love is just hormones.

BRANDON: Just hormones?

SLOANE: It's so we'll make babies. Our DNA has to replicate itself, that's all.

BRANDON: You think the hormones make you *believe* you're in love?

SLOANE: Exactly, *Somerset Maugham*/

BRANDON: Ohmygod/

SLOANE: —said "Love's a dirty trick played on us to achieve continuation of the species."

BRANDON: *(Groans)* Somerset Maugham?

SLOANE: My favorite writer!

BRANDON: So love doesn't exist?

SLOANE: No, it exists. But it's temporary, *transitory*, it doesn't last and then everybody just gets divorced anyway.

BRANDON: Well, everything is temporary, life is temporary, that doesn't mean we shouldn't live it! What you're saying sounds so *clinical* and, and besides, Sloane, you're a beautiful gal. You're in the… springtime of your life. Where's the romance?

SLOANE: Romance. Uggh. Romance is so…*narcissistic.* Brandon, it's very simple. I have no interest in getting married, I've always felt that way, I don't even like guys to spend the night…as you know…but I do want to have a baby and I want to pick the sperm, that's all. It's not such a big deal.

BRANDON: The *father* Sloane, the *Dad*, it's a huge deal.

SLOANE: I'm just trying to organize my life Brandon. I don't want any surprises.

BRANDON: Look, I think it's clear that I'm not comfortable with this. And offering me money makes me feel creepy, frankly. Like, you're impugning my honor.

SLOANE: Your what?

BRANDON: My honor, Sloane, my honor!

SLOANE: I'm not paying you to…to *date* me, God! It wouldn't change anything. We could still, you know, hang out.

BRANDON: You're wrong, it would change things. It would change everything.

SLOANE: You're totally over-thinking this Brandon, it's a *business* transaction.

BRANDON: Also I…I can't do the Yip thing on Friday, there's this thing at school—

SLOANE: No. NO!

BRANDON: It's an Open House, I really should be there.

SLOANE: But you said yes to me—that's not fair.

BRANDON: I'm sorry Sloane but you can find someone else.

SLOANE: No, I can't, it's too late—

BRANDON: Yes, you can. If anyone can, you can.

SLOANE: You can't quit on me! That's being TOTALLY irresponsible!

BRANDON: Sloane, I said I'm sorry but I have to be at school, that's my first priority, it's my job.

SLOANE: Open Houses are so dumb, the parents just wander around and look at dopey projects—

BRANDON: Thanks Sloane, thanks a lot.

SLOANE: I didn't mean, that was stupid— *(Gesturing to wall)* —I mean, this is *amazing/*

BRANDON: Look, maybe we should take a little break.

SLOANE: What? A break? A break? Historically *I* always do the breaking up.

BRANDON: Step back a little. Get some room.

SLOANE: Fine! Take all the room you want but I *will* send over the tux and you *will be* my model.

BRANDON: NO! I'm not doing it, Sloane, forget it. I'm *out.*

SLOANE: Great, this is what I get for going out with a guy I met at *House of Brews.*

BRANDON: You picked me up!

SLOANE: I did NOT! You are soooo dumb!

BRANDON: Fine, I'm dumb, really mature Sloane.

SLOANE: You're probably teaching them that the world is flat, huh, aren't you? Huh?

BRANDON: Sloane, that is so ridiculous. Really, you should leave.

SLOANE: You said you'd do something and now—

BRANDON: And now I can't. I am NOT going to do it!

SLOANE: It's an important show, Yip is important!

BRANDON: I'm sure he's *very* important.

SLOANE: God, you make me so mad, you are such a jerk!

BRANDON: I know Sloane, now please go.

SLOANE: *Such* a jerk—

BRANDON: LEAVE!

SLOANE: (*Gesturing to all the pictures of the Presidents*) And they…and *they* think you're a jerk too! (*She slams the door and exits.*)

(*Blackout*)

Scene Four

(*Later that afternoon*)

(DOUG *and* BRANDON*'s apartment. The front door is wide open.*)

(DOUG*'s in front of his laptop playing World of Warcraft.*)

(*Towards the end of his monologue* SLOANE *appears, holding* BRANDON*'s tux.*)

DOUG: (*Talking to the screen*) Hot it up, okay hot it up, you can do it, just hang on, you're gonna get through, okay, okay more buff, more buff, MORE BUFF YOU MOTHERFUCKER, good, good, WATCH THE FUCKING SUCCUBUS, yes piss me, piss ME! Imp posse FUCK ME, you pussies, you pussies you fucking imp posse pussies come to mommy, yes, yes, KITE IT, KITE it, in the crapper goodbye you are so fucking dumb. No, no, those fucking GNOMES, I hate those fucking gnomes, okay, okay, fel guards, fel guards on left, on left…hang on, hang on, okay increase the d.p.s and level the a.b.s., level the a.b.s., ALL RIGHT I'M IN THE BACK DOOR, FUCK THE GNOMES. Not gonna go back to hearth, no way Jose, can't go go back to hearth, no way you fucking gnomes, coming at you from behind/

SLOANE: Hello?

DOUG: YES, YES, I PONE ZORED YES!

SLOANE: Hel-lo!

DOUG: I PONE ZORED YOU!

SLOANE: Brandon?

DOUG: *(Sees* SLOANE*)* Shit!

(SLOANE *and* DOUG *both scream.)*

DOUG: You scared me! Sorry! God! Sorry. Hi, umm, hello.

(DOUG *is struck by* SLOANE*'s beauty.)*

SLOANE: Oh, sorry. Is this Brandon Fitzgerald's apartment? The super said…

DOUG: Yeah, yeah, he lives here.

SLOANE: Oh. Do you live here? Are you his roommate?

DOUG: Yeah, I live here. I'm his brother.

SLOANE: His *brother?*

DOUG: I'm Doug.

SLOANE: You're his *brother?*

DOUG: We had the same parents? You know, beat each other up in the car…

SLOANE: Oh, I'm sorry, I didn't know he had a brother.

DOUG: Yeah, I'm Doug the Brother! Come on *down!*

(DOUG *gestures for* SLOANE *to come in but she doesn't budge.)*

SLOANE: The door was wide open. Carlos let me in.

DOUG: Well come on in! Wanna play?

SLOANE: No thanks. What is that?

DOUG: W.O.W. World of Warcraft.

SLOANE: You sounded so…expert.

DOUG: Practice. Commitment. Dedication. Pedal to the Metal. Nose to the Grindstone. Shoulder to the plow.

SLOANE: Right. Uh, huh. Is, is Brandon here?

DOUG: No, it's just me and all my other personalities, blaaah.

SLOANE: Oh, God!

DOUG: Hey hey, sorry, just goofing around. Whadd'ya say your name was again?

SLOANE: I'm…ah, S… *Liz*. SLiz. Liz Novak. So nice to meet you. I'm supposed to drop off a tux for Brandon.

DOUG: Seriously, c'mon on in. I don't bite. Only at mealtimes!

(SLOANE *tentatively walks in the room and hangs the tux on a hook on the wall.*)

SLOANE: Maybe I'll just leave it here. (*She turns to go.*)

DOUG: Hey, don't go. A tux, whoa, what's the deal?

SLOANE: He's gonna be in the Yip Yardley fashion show.

DOUG: He's gonna be in a fashion show?

SLOANE: He's like an escort.

DOUG: (*Shocked*) No way!

(SLOANE *laughs, and notices the recycling.*)

SLOANE: Wow, did you have a big party here last night? (*Points to the recycling bin full to the brim with empty beer cans.*)

DOUG: Nah, that's just the recycling.

SLOANE: The living room's an interesting place to put it.

DOUG: Well yeah, it makes sense. (*Takes an empty from the coffee table, throws it into the bin and makes it.*) SCORE, HE SCORES! TWO POINTS you sissies!

SLOANE: It's just that most people put it in the kitchen.

DOUG: Yeah, so what?

SLOANE: It kinda makes *more* sense in the kitchen.

DOUG: Well, I think it makes *more* sense here.

SLOANE: (*Sees POGO and heads for the aquarium*) Oh my God, you have a… (*Peers into aquarium*) …what is he, is he a Bearded Dragon? I have a Leopard Gecko! Oh, look, he's in his little house, he's so *adorable*, what's his name?

DOUG: That's Pogo.

SLOANE: That's perfect because he's a Pogona lizard!

DOUG: Wow, you know a lot, nobody knows that.

SLOANE: I love reptiles.

DOUG: Jeez.

SLOANE: Do you feed him crickets too? That's mostly what Lucca eats, my gecko. And do you coat the crickets with calcium, that's *very* important.

DOUG: Yeah, I think so. Buffer usually feeds him.

SLOANE: Buffer? Buffer?

DOUG: Somethin' to drink?

SLOANE: Sparkling water?

DOUG: Ah…I got water.

SLOANE: That's fine.

(DOUG *exits to get water and* SLOANE *looks around.*)

DOUG: (*From kitchen*) You met Carlos?

SLOANE: Yeah, really nice guy.

DOUG: He can bench press like three fifty, it's awesome. *(He enters and points to the box of Captain Crunch that he's holding.)* Cereal?

SLOANE: No, thank you. So, where do you work?

(DOUG hands SLOANE her glass of water.)

DOUG: Right now I work at a fruit stand. Got off early today. But I'm probably gonna go back to school soon.

SLOANE: You left?

DOUG: I had an accident. TBI. Traumatic brain injury. Good days, bad days.

SLOANE: What happened?

DOUG: I hit a tree.

SLOANE: A car accident?

DOUG: No, in my fraternity.

SLOANE: You hit a tree in your fraternity?

DOUG: No, I jumped out of a window, bounced off a pile of mattresses on the ground and *then* I hit a tree.

SLOANE: Bummer.

DOUG: Yeah, I don't know why I did it. I was wasted. Everyone was cheering, the whole school was there, it was like this *wave*, I was on this wave and I was like… I'm superman!

SLOANE: And then…boom.

DOUG: Right? There was a fight about where to take me, you know, which hospital? Some bros wanted to say I fell in a barn in the country or something, so the frat wouldn't get in trouble. You know, so the university wouldn't shut us down. Afterwards they called me. *(He pauses for effect.)* The Defenestrator.

SLOANE: *The Defenestrator?* You're like a legend then.

DOUG: I don't know. I only really see one guy from then. He told me about *The Defenestrator* deal.

SLOANE: Just one guy?

DOUG: Yeah, the other bros, they're like on to other stuff you know.

(Pause)

SLOANE: Where'd you go?

DOUG: Cornell.

SLOANE: Cornell! I went there! Well, for a—

DOUG: No way! When did you go?

SLOANE: Oh…ages ago.

DOUG: I bet I was there way before you.

SLOANE: And…I transferred.

DOUG: You *transferred?* You hated it?

SLOANE: No, I didn't hate it. I just…you know, the partying.

DOUG: Yeah, you were like hardcore, huh?

SLOANE: *(She laughs nervously)* Well, like I thought I could handle it and that I was, you know, *invincible* but like one morning I knew I had to go. Period. I *had* to go. So I left.

DOUG: Intense.

SLOANE: Yeah.

DOUG: Where'd you transfer?

SLOANE: Dartmouth.

DOUG: Camp Dartmouth? Are you crazy?

SLOANE: I know, it's insane.

DOUG: You left Cornell because of the partying? But Dartmouth is like one big rage!

SLOANE: But my Mom and Dad went there. My Grandpa. I felt more…I don't know, at home.

DOUG: That is whacked. From the frying pan into the… toaster? What's that expression?

SLOANE: Into the fire. From the frying pan into the fire. You're funny.

DOUG: You're funny. Dartmouth. *(Sarcastic) Not* a party school.

SLOANE: Well, I learned. At Cornell. What *not* to do.

(Pause)

DOUG: Alpha Delt.

SLOANE: Of course you were in AD, Mr Defenestrator.

DOUG: Right. Yeah, hey, I'm sorry you didn't have a good time.

SLOANE: No, it's fine. All good.

(A pause while the wild frat world descends for a moment.)

SLOANE: So, do your parents, uh, live in the city?

DOUG: Just Buffer. Mom's upstate and Dad's in Mass.

SLOANE: What's he do?

DOUG: Mechanic. When he works.

SLOANE: *When* he works?

DOUG: Hits the sauce. Loves the juice.

SLOANE: Great. Great. So, do you have a girlfriend? I bet you have a girlfriend.

DOUG: Nah, I don't have a girlfriend…

SLOANE: Does your brother have a girlfriend?

DOUG: A ton.

SLOANE: A *ton?*

DOUG: I mean he sees a lot of girls, he doesn't have like a *real* girlfriend. More like a *harem*.

SLOANE: A *harem*? So he goes out with a lot of girls?

DOUG: Oh, yeah. Real babe magnet.

SLOANE: Have you ever met any of them?

DOUG: Nope. God, you should work for the CIA!

SLOANE: So, do like you and your brother meet girls over here?

DOUG: I wish we had girls over her, jeez, bring em' on.

SLOANE: I mean, the panties on the wall, that's cute. You probably have wild parties sometimes, right? *(Points to the pair of panties on the wall)*

DOUG: In my dreams.

SLOANE: Oh c'mon Doug, I'm not an idiot.

DOUG: I should have a big rage here, really.

SLOANE: *(Upset)* Rage on, yeah, rage on!

DOUG: Hey, are you okay? You don't look right.

SLOANE: I am fine, I am totally fine, I have never been finer, really. I am someone who likes to know things, I'm not afraid to *know* things, I'm not afraid to *face* things, to know the truth, I am a truth seeker really—

DOUG: You need a beer man, lemme get you a beer.

SLOANE: I mean, I don't care about your little FRAT parties, really I could care less—

DOUG: No no no—oh, no.

(There's a knock on the door.)

SLOANE: Well, you're popular today. Could that be your brother, Buffer? Any chance that the famous brother will show up? I am going to fucking kill him—

DOUG: Nah, he wouldn't knock. *(Goes to door)* It's probably the old lady next door. She always smells gas and I have to go sniff.

(DOUG opens door and KATERINA is standing there.)

KATERINA: Doug? *(Pronounced Duck)* Douglas? *(Pronounced Duck-glass)* Fitzgerald?

DOUG: Yeah, that's me. Oh. Oh, dude.

KATERINA: Arthur tell you I come?

SLOANE: This should be good.

KATERINA: *(Flirtatiously, thinking that SLOANE is part of the call, walks over to her)* Hello! I am Katerina.

SLOANE: Hi. I'm S…Liz, Liz Novak.

(KATERINA checks out SLOANE.)

KATERINA: Are you Douglas girlfriend? Arthur didn't say he had girlfriend. Oh, I like the threesome. I very good with ladies.

SLOANE: *(Horrified)* No! No! I have to go, I'm just visiting, I have to go soon/

KATERINA: *(Understanding now)* Ohhhh!

(SLOANE and KATERINA laugh together.)

KATERINA: *(Stroking SLOANE's leather bag)* I love your bag! What bag is that?

SLOANE: Oh! It's Bottega Veneta.

KATERINA: Very beautiful. Very.

SLOANE: So, you're a friend of Buffer's too?

KATERINA: Buffer? Who is that? *(Looks at DOUG)* You are Duck-glass, right?

DOUG: Yeah, yeah I'm Duck-glass, yahoo! Buffer's my brother…you don't know him.

KATERINA: *(Back to bag)* Soft like bottom of the baby!

SLOANE: Thank you. I've had it for *ages*.

DOUG: *(To* KATERINA*)* Do you want something to drink, I got beer, wine…

KATERINA: You have maybe the sparkling water?

DOUG: *(Looking at* SLOANE*)* No…but I'm thinking about getting some.

KATERINA: Beer very nice. I like the Bud Lite.

DOUG: The Bud Lite. *(Runs to frig to get her a Bud Lite)* I think I left the bath running. Liz, I'll be right back.

*(*DOUG *hands* KATERINA *a beer and exits.)*

KATERINA: *(Looking at* SLOANE*)* So, how pretty are you! Are you Polish?

SLOANE: Sure. Novak. Right. My *Dad* is Polish, my mother is…Swedish.

KATERINA: Oh, very nice, I like the Swedish, very nice the Swedish. Polish, I am sorry.

SLOANE: And you're Russian?

KATERINA: No! I am Estonian. Near the Russia. *(Looking very closely at* SLOANE*)* You have very good skin, how do you say, no…little holes…

SLOANE: Pores. No pores.

KATERINA: I remember. *Pores.* So, you are very rich?

SLOANE: Yes. You're so funny, no one ever *asks*.

KATERINA: Good, I marry you. Just kidding. Rich and beautiful. You are very easy to love. Many mens will love you.

SLOANE: I'm not really very lovable.

KATERINA: Girls like you…very easy to catch a man. But not so easy to keep sometime.

SLOANE: Really, why's that?

KATERINA: You ever see ugly woman with good-looking husband?

SLOANE: Yeah.

KATERINA: She not worry about *why* he love her, *if* he love her for right reason like beautiful women worry. She just treat him nice. All the time! She listen, she say honey your cock is best cock in whole world.

SLOANE: You are *so* funny.

KATERINA: I very smart. Some day I have designer bag like you.

SLOANE: I bet you will.

(DOUG *enters running, slides on his socks and strikes a pose in his new clothes: a button-down shirt over his T-shirt and new shorts, very suave.*)

SLOANE: Doug, I gotta run.

(SLOANE *holds out her hand to* KATERINA)

SLOANE: Katerina, it was soo nice to meet you.

DOUG: Yeah, well, thanks for bringing the tux. I'm gonna give the Buffman some grief.

SLOANE: Yeah, go for it.

(*As* SLOANE *goes:*)

KATERINA: Bye, bye, I hope I see you again Liz! I like you very much even if you have the Polish! (*Turning to* DOUG) Hello again. Someday I buy nice bag like she has. (*Takes off her coat, revealing a very sexy outfit*)

DOUG: What was your name again?

KATERINA: Katerina. Tushenko.

DOUG: Great! Katerina Tushenko. Cool. I'm gonna call you "Tush!" You Russian, Tush?

KATERINA: No! I'm from Estonia! You know the Estonia?

DOUG: No.

KATERINA: Don't worry, no one knows the Estonia.

DOUG: Wanna cookie? I got cookies.

KATERINA: No, the sweets, they hate me, thank you. Opps! *(She falls back on chair.)* Duck-glass, come sit. Arthur says you have birthday.

DOUG: Yeah, tomorrow. *(He sits next to her on chair.)*

KATERINA: You big man.

DOUG: *(Transfixed)* Yeah.

KATERINA: You look very nice in the shorts.

DOUG: I get hot. You know. Easily.

KATERINA: So tell me what for birthday you want?

DOUG: *(He is overwhelmed)* Where, where are you from again?

KATERINA: Tallinn, a big city in the Estonia. Near the Russia.

DOUG: Tell me about that. About when you were a little kid there.

KATERINA: But we have only one hour, Duck.

DOUG: Yeah, let's talk first.

KATERINA: You want talk now?

DOUG: Is that alright?

KATERINA: Yes, Arthur told me you had accident.

DOUG: Yeah.

KATERINA: But you getting better?

DOUG: I am, I really am.

KATERINA: *(Makes a motion near her groin)* So, everything all…work okay?

DOUG: Oh, yeah, it works. I, ah…keep it in good shape.

KATERINA: Good, then no problem!

(KATERINA *pulls her top over her head, revealing a very sexy camisole.* DOUG *rushes to cover her up.*)

DOUG: But I'm a little…well, it's been awhile, you know, with somebody.

KATERINA: So?

DOUG: So let's just…*chat* for now, okay?

KATERINA: Chat? You want just chat?

DOUG: That would be great.

KATERINA: Okay, I very good at chat.

(*Pause while* DOUG *and* KATERINA *look at each other.*)

KATERINA: What we chat about?

(DOUG *and* KATERINA *think.*)

(*Blackout*)

Scene Five

(*Afternoon, after school*)

(BRANDON's *classroom. He's grading papers. His phone buzzes, he reads the text, and ignores it. He works some more.*)

(*There's a knock on his closed door, the door opens and* SLOANE *enters.* BRANDON *looks up. She is angry.*)

SLOANE: Well hello.

BRANDON: (*Startled*) Hello—Sloane.

SLOANE: I texted you, you didn't text me back.

BRANDON: We broke up, Sloane.

SLOANE: No. No.

BRANDON: Yes!

SLOANE: We will break up, when I get a few answers to a few questions—

BRANDON: You don't get to have questions. We broke up.

SLOANE: Well, I do have questions, *Buffer.*

(*Pause*)

BRANDON: What did you say?

SLOANE: Well *Buffer,* I said I'm really curious about a few facts of your life, *Buffer.*

BRANDON: Why do you keep calling me that?

SLOANE: That's what your brother calls you.

BRANDON: What? My brother?

SLOANE: Yeah, Doug, your brother.

BRANDON: How do you know about my brother?

SLOANE: I went to your apartment this afternoon, I thought you lived alone—

BRANDON: You went to my apartment? Today?

SLOANE: I was just gonna drop the tux off with Carlos like you said—

BRANDON: So you met Doug?

SLOANE: More or less.

BRANDON: Either you met him or you didn't.

SLOANE: Okay I did, I met him, but he thinks I'm *Liz.*

BRANDON: Who's Liz?

SLOANE: She works in my office.

BRANDON: So you went to my apartment, you met my brother and you told him you were some other person?

SLOANE: It was an accident. I didn't mean to meet him. Why don't you want me to anyway?

BRANDON: Sloane, this is all getting too bizarre for me. You're impersonating other people, going to my apartment, this is stalking behavior! This is why we should take a break. We aren't even taking a break. We're broken up!

SLOANE: That's ridiculous.

BRANDON: It's not ridiculous!

SLOANE: We're having a good time/

BRANDON: We *were* having a good time/

SLOANE: And all that bullshit about your parents was a total lie.

BRANDON: Listen Sloane, I gotta finish these papers and—

SLOANE: Your Father is *not* an engineer, he fixes cars!

BRANDON: He *was* an engineer. There's nothing *wrong* with being a mechanic.

SLOANE: When he's not *tanked!*

BRANDON: And what about your father? You're always saying what a drunk he is!

SLOANE: Daddy is a very functional alcoholic!

BRANDON: Great! Terrific.

SLOANE: And your pad was just like a frat…all ready to entertain the babes! Where was the bowl of condoms, huh?

BRANDON: I mean it, you should leave now.

SLOANE: Doug said you have lots of girlfriends.

BRANDON: So?

SLOANE: *Tons* is how he put it.

BRANDON: So what? What's the deal here? Why are you acting all jealous?

SLOANE: And then this Estonian girl showed up, I mean obviously she was a prostitute.

BRANDON: She is not a prostitute, she's an escort.

SLOANE: You know about her?

BRANDON: It's hard for him to meet girls and he…. Christ, I don't have to justify this. He's my big brother!

SLOANE: I can't believe I'm involved with someone who hires *escorts*!

BRANDON: We're not *involved*!

SLOANE: Brandon, you never told me you had a *brother*!

BRANDON: Sloane, this is strange, I mean I've known you for about…three weeks!

SLOANE: Three months! We've known each other for three months! Where have you been?!

BRANDON: …and this conversation is starting to feel like we're married or something!

SLOANE: Oh? Really? It does?

BRANDON: Yeah.

SLOANE: Well, you're the one who started yelling.

BRANDON: You're the one who went to my apartment—

SLOANE: I was dropping off the tux!

BRANDON: —and interrogated my brother!

SLOANE: We had a very nice chat. He liked me and I liked him!

BRANDON: Doug likes everyone. It's the positive side of brain-damage.

SLOANE: He's not brain-damaged.

BRANDON: Oh, I'm not getting into that with you/

SLOANE: He's not brain-damaged! No, he's funny and maybe he's a little…traumatized.

BRANDON: You don't know anything.

SLOANE: And why wouldn't he be after what he went through in that horrible frat? Those dickwads. Really. And then they make a big joke of it—The Defenestrator.

BRANDON: The Defenestrator.

SLOANE: That slays me, I'm hysterical. The Defenestrator.

(Beat)

BRANDON: He told you all that?

SLOANE: Yeah. He did. We definitely hit it off.

BRANDON: I guess.

SLOANE: And I met Pogo. Your Bearded Dragon.

BRANDON: Yeah, Pogo, so?

SLOANE: So, I have a gecko.

BRANDON: You have a *pet*?

SLOANE: You're not very observant. Lucca. I've had him since high school. He's very sweet.

BRANDON: Sweet?

SLOANE: And kind and understanding. So, anyway. Are we done here? We're taking a break? You're breaking up with me?

BRANDON: No, historically *you* do the breaking up…

SLOANE: Yeah, historically that's true. *(Pause)* So, I guess, have a great life Brandon. *(She goes to the door.)*

BRANDON: Why'd you name him Lucca?

SLOANE: It's my favorite city in Italy.

BRANDON: How come?

SLOANE: It's very medieval, like a fairy tale. The city has walls from the sixteenth century all around it and you're not allowed to drive a car in the center.

BRANDON: Cool.

SLOANE: Yeah, you have to walk or bike, it's really neat.

BRANDON: Sounds awesome.

(*Pause while* BRANDON *and* SLOANE *consider one another.*)

SLOANE: So you hate me now, right?

BRANDON: No, I don't hate you. I mean, you're crazy Sloane but you're, you're…

SLOANE: What? I'm what?

BRANDON: Well you're definitely not boring, and you're very, you know…*Sloane-like.*

SLOANE: Thank you.

BRANDON: I'll be about an hour or so. You heading home?

SLOANE: Probably.

BRANDON: You want me to come over?

SLOANE: Maybe.

BRANDON: Maybe?

SLOANE: Sure, come on over.

BRANDON: But you can't talk about my sperm, okay? It's a serious downer.

SLOANE: (*Walking towards* BRANDON) But it's because I—

BRANDON: That's the rule, Sloane! That's my one rule.

SLOANE: Okay! Okay. I have a rule too.

(SLOANE *leans into* BRANDON *more, he inhales her hair.*)

BRANDON: Do you?

SLOANE: I do. And here it is. Just give everyone an A.

(SLOANE *hands* BRANDON *a pen. They look at each other for a moment, then she slowly exits. He gets her point, quickly grabs his papers and follows after her.)*

(Blackout)

Scene Six

(The next day)

(DOUG *and* BRANDON'*s apartment)*

(KATERINA *is standing holding a container of soup and a paper bag with bread in it.* DOUG *has just let her in.)*

KATERINA: So, I brought for you the *schi,* the soup of cabbage, that my Baba cooks. You said you want, remember? And today your birthday, yes? Happy Birthday!

DOUG: Yeah, it is, jeez, that is so nice, Tush!

KATERINA: And this we call the *full schi* because in it is all the parts, everything that in a real *schi* is. Yes, we have the beef, the onion, the cabbage, the cream that is sour of course, you know, the whole kitty noodle.

DOUG: Kitty noodle?

KATERINA: Yes, kitty noodle. Everything, the carrots, the potatoes, the garlic…*many* garlics.

DOUG: Kitty noodle, kitty noodle. Wait, you mean kit and *kaboodle,* that's what you mean, we say kit and *kaboodle.* Kit and *kaboodle.*

KATERINA: Kit and kanoodle?

DOUG: Kit and *kaboodle!* But I like kitty noodle better!

KATERINA: So, I brought for you. And black Russian bread. And Duck-glass, when you have soup you take slice of tomato, put in bottom of bowl and pour hot soup over. Soup cook tomato and you eat with black Russian bread, you make dipping in soup, very good.

DOUG: Make dipping. Gee, thanks. *(Walks towards kitchen)* I'll put it in the kitchen, this is a *huge* apartment.

KATERINA: *(Calling after him)* Duck! From you I need a favor, okay?

DOUG: Sure, what? *(He comes back into the room.)*

KATERINA: Okay, so I'm at the Bocca del Lupo where I am hostess, you know seventy-six and the Lex? and last night nice man come in, sit at bar, Armani suit, looks very good, his teeth they are very white. So we talk, and he tells me he loves the tennis! I tell him I love too! Then he says "play with me next Saturday at club on Long Island, okay?" I say "Okay!" So now I need to learn the tennis, can you teach? He works at the Goldman Sachs!

DOUG: So, you like this guy? You want to go out with him?

KATERINA: Duck-glass. I want to go to school, become crime scene examiner. Blood, murder—no problem. But I need money to go to school and I want my own apartment! My roommate, Svetlana, she meet a man on the Wall Street, Teddy, and Teddy send her to school, buy her *Prada,* Teddy is very good to her and I need a Teddy too. Svetlana is so disgusting, last night she ate whole cooked chicken standing up with her fingers! She gross me out.

DOUG: You want to marry him, Mr White Teeth?

KATERINA: He *is* married. I not want to be married Duck!

DOUG: Ever?

KATERINA: For green card maybe.

DOUG: You don't have your green card?

KATERINA: The agency try to get for me.

DOUG: The agency?

KATERINA: The modeling agency that bring me from Tallinn.

DOUG: I'll marry you if you need a green card.

KATERINA: Duck-glass! You need to fall in love, then marry, this is America!

DOUG: I love you.

KATERINA: Duck, you very sweet, but you don't love me!

DOUG: Yes I do.

KATERINA: That's crazy!

DOUG: Yup, I'm crazy. It's mad.

KATERINA: But you don't know me!

DOUG: Sure I do.

KATERINA: I am terrible Estonian bimbo who want to find rich American who buy her fancy clothes and go to fancy restaurants and spend all his money!

DOUG: You can spend all my money!

KATERINA: *(Looking around and gesturing)* Duck-glass, you are not rich!

DOUG: I might be.

KATERINA: You are me kidding.

DOUG: No, I have a baseball card that could be valuable, I kid you not. *(He runs to get the box of baseball cards.)* My Dad gave me his old collection and I was looking at it and there's one in there that may be worth a ton. You know baseball?

KATERINA: Of course! Grand slam. Home run! Curse of the Bambino!

DOUG: *(Looking in box)* So I have this card. Napolean Lajolie. They called him The Nap.

(DOUG *hands* KATERINA *The Nap.)*

KATERINA: *(Looking at card)* And this card sell for very much money?

DOUG: Well, the internet said it was super valuable but you can't always trust the internet. But I might be a very rich dude.

KATERINA: For just one baseball card?

DOUG: Well, maybe. I'm gonna research it more.

KATERINA: *(Thinking)* I have cousin, Sergei, he's been here long time and he sell comic book, card like you have of baseball, old posters, he would know. His shop in Queens near me! You want me to ask?

DOUG: Ask him how much I could get for it?

KATERINA: Sure, he do that for free!

DOUG: Maybe.

KATERINA: Don't you want to know how much?

DOUG: Sure, but…

KATERINA: Sergei very good.

DOUG: I dunno.

KATERINA: Oh…you don't trust me?

DOUG: No, no, I totally trust you. I should just ask Buffer.

KATERINA: You want to come with me to Sergei's shop?

DOUG: No, I just…I did such a stupid thing, did Arthur tell you the stupid thing I did?

KATERINA: No, just that you had accident at your college.

DOUG: I jumped out a window for a *joke*, a joke--I like ruined my life.

KATERINA: No, no, you had a very bad thing happen, but this is everyone. It's not all your life, just a little piece! You are here afraid, that is not good Duck. You can't sit here forever.

DOUG: I fucked up so bad.

KATERINA: That is over now, forget it! We have today and tomorrow Duck. Today and tomorrow.

DOUG: You are great Tush.

KATERINA: No, I am bad I have done many stupid things too like you. But I have not jumped out a window. Yet. When you are ready I ask Sergei.

(KATERINA *hands The Nap back to* DOUG.)

KATERINA: Not until then.

(DOUG *looks at The Nap while* KATERINA *gets her coat on. After a couple of beats he speaks.*)

DOUG: I'm ready, you're right, I can't sit here forever. This might be worth something, I should know what it's worth.

(KATERINA *reaches under her shirt and unclasps a piece of jewelry, a locket, and shows it to* DOUG.)

KATERINA: This my Baba gave me. Real gold, real pearls. If someone has gun on head I do not give. You keep if you want to give me card for Sergei.

DOUG: No, you don't have to do that.

KATERINA: NO! I not take card unless you take this.

(KATERINA *puts locket in* DOUG'*s hands.*)

(DOUG *hands her The Nap.*)

DOUG: See. He was probably the best second baseman of all time.

KATERINA: He is so handsome!

(DOUG *and* KATERINA *laugh.)*

KATERINA: So I show Sergei tonight and bring back tomorrow. You teach me the tennis okay?

DOUG: Okay, great!

KATERINA: I see tennis court in Riverside Park. We play for free. Five o'clock, yes? I come here.

DOUG: Sure, five o'clock.

(KATERINA *slips The Nap inside her bra.)*

KATERINA: I keep it very safe, right here. Very safe.

(Blackout)

Scene Seven

(Late that night. DOUG *and* BRANDON's *apartment.)*

BRANDON: Okay, lemme get this straight, you gave…

DOUG: Katerina, her name is Katerina.

BRANDON: You gave the hooker—

DOUG: She's my *friend.* You got her for me!

BRANDON: You gave your hooker friend—

DOUG: Fuck you!

BRANDON: Anyway, you gave her some stupid baseball card that you think is worth something. Like anything Dad gave us would be worth anything.

DOUG: It could be worth a hundred grand, I looked it up on the internet.

BRANDON: What? Gimme a break.

DOUG: I told you and you said I was full of shit.

BRANDON: You never told me that.

DOUG: I told you *multiple times* but you blew me off.

BRANDON: Alright, alright. Sorry.

DOUG: And then I forgot about it until I was gonna make Pogo like a couch and I was looking for a shoebox and… *(Holds up box)* Voila. All the cards.

BRANDON: Okay, what is it again? *(He opens his computer.)*

DOUG: The Nap. Napolean Lajoie. L.A.J.O.I.E.

BRANDON: Lajoie, what kind of name is…holy shit. *(Reading from computer)* "Originally left out of the 1933 Goudey set, this card was only available to collectors who wrote in to request it. Forty to fifty thousand. If autographed could be worth over twice the value." Holy fucking shit! You never told me this dude!

DOUG: I did man, I did. You weren't listening as per usual, sometimes you don't listen bro.

BRANDON: And you gave it to her?

DOUG: She has a cousin in Queens who sells comics and cards and he'll give us a free *estimate!*

BRANDON: Slow down. Seriously, go back—you gave, whatsherface, *Katrina*—

DOUG: *Katerina!*

BRANDON: You tell me this thing is valuable and you just gave it to her?

DOUG: This is a great thing! You always tell me to get off my ass, so I did! Listen! You can talk to her tomorrow! She's coming over! We're gonna play tennis!

BRANDON: It's a scam Doug, you're not getting a free fucking estimate, she scammed you!

DOUG: No! She gave me this locket her Baba gave her, see… *(He pulls it out of his pocket.)* … it's real gold and it's like, you know…what's that word…so I would trust her.

BRANDON: Collateral. Bullshit. Of course she gave you her "Baba" thing that she bought yesterday on Fourteenth Street…of *course* she did. She's schooled in this shit dude. She's, she's…a hooker!

DOUG: She's a model! That's how she got here, a modeling agency brought her over/

BRANDON: A hooker—

DOUG: Model—

BRANDON: HOOKER!

DOUG: SHE'S A MODEL! And I love her! She brought me soup for my birthday.

BRANDON: Maybe we should call the police.

DOUG: NO! We are not calling the police, no.

BRANDON: The longer we wait the harder it'll be for them to find her.

DOUG: She'll be back, you asshole, she will—

BRANDON: In your dreams buddy, in your dreams—

DOUG: *Fuck* you.

BRANDON: Fuck *you*. This is so royally fucked. Now, when we *really* need the money, it's unbelievable. Unfucking unbelievable.

DOUG: I thought you said we were okay, that's why you didn't want to sell your sperms.

BRANDON: We're not okay now.

DOUG: What happened?

BRANDON: The insurance dude. I got a call, now Mom's place is only half covered, we gotta come up with the other half.

DOUG: Shit. That's like, how much?

BRANDON: I gotta find her another place, that's how much.

DOUG: We'll sell the Nap, Buff, we'll sell it.

BRANDON: A, we don't have it and B, we don't know what it's worth!

DOUG: But we will when we get the estimate, it's gotta be worth something.

BRANDON: The Nap is gone dude, where is your brain! *(Pause)* I'm sorry Doug, I didn't mean—

DOUG: Yes, well, that is the question. Where is my brain?

BRANDON: You're fine Doug, you're doing great, you know that, really great. *(Pause)* Did you check out all the other cards?

DOUG: Yeah. Nuthin'. But you can try. Or call Dad.

BRANDON: I am *not* gonna call Dad.

DOUG: He'd want them all back if he thought they were worth anything.

BRANDON: Fuck that. I don't believe this.

DOUG: Katerina did not steal The Nap. She will be back. She will.

BRANDON: Right.

DOUG: But if you're worried, sell your love potion! To that girl—what's her name?

BRANDON: Sloane. Doug, we've been through this.

DOUG: The money's on the table! What's the big deal?

BRANDON: It is a huge deal, it is an enormous deal. If I give her my sperm she may use it and get pregnant and have a real live PERSON and I would be the real live FATHER. That's the big fucking deal.

DOUG: Just do it, you wanna control everything, you're like a control freak.

BRANDON: I am not a control freak!

DOUG: You are! You flip out when I put the recycling in here, who the fuck cares! You are so fucking UPTIGHT.

BRANDON: It's STUPID to have the recycling in here, it's just STUPID. And I am not uptight, I'm trying to take care of shit Doug! If she has a kid I'm the father, that's the FACT. Someday some angry teenager could show up and say hey dude, you're my fucking father, you've got weird eyebrows and long fingers just like me and what would I say? Huh? I can't do that so get off my case! I'm not, I'm NOT gonna sell my sperm to Sloane. No, no, no, NO!

(Silence)

DOUG: I think the word is sperms dude, *sperms. (He exits.)*

(Blackout)

Scene Eight

(DOUG and BRANDON's apartment. DOUG is all cleaned up, in his tennis whites. He hears a knock on the door and races to answer it.)

DOUG: Helloooo.

(DOUG opens the door. SLOANE in standing there, all dressed up.)

DOUG: *(Disappointed)* Oh. Liz.

SLOANE: Liz. Right. Hi. Hey, what's wrong?

DOUG: I'm sorry, I thought you were someone else.

SLOANE: *(Motioning to his clothes) You* look like someone else!

DOUG: Yeah, I'm just waiting for Katerina…

SLOANE: The Estonian girl?

DOUG: …we're gonna play tennis.

SLOANE: Yeah, I see.

DOUG: Hey, I've got sparkling water, want some?

SLOANE: Yes, please.

*(*DOUG *goes to kitchen.* SLOANE *calls after him.)*

SLOANE: I came to pick up the tux. Brandon bailed.

*(*DOUG *comes back in with a bottle of sparkling water.)*

DOUG: Yeah, whatawuss.

*(*DOUG *hands* SLOANE *the water.)*

DOUG: One sparkling.

SLOANE: So, you and Katerina are gonna play tennis?

DOUG: Yeah, at five.

*(*BRANDON *enters with just a towel around his waist.)*

BRANDON: Dude, did you pick up the dry… *(He sees* SLOANE *and stops talking.)* Sloane! Hey! Hey, what's up, you look so nice.

SLOANE: Thank you. Just here to pick up the tux, sorry.

BRANDON: No, totally. I get it. *(Kidding)* But I thought I'd wear it for the Open House.

SLOANE: Yeah, yeah. *Justin's* gonna to it, you know that *doctor* from Columbia? He's *da bomb.*

BRANDON: I told you so.

SLOANE: Brandon.

BRANDON: Sloane.

DOUG: Buffer. *(Pause)* This is *Liz*.

BRANDON: Sloane, why don't you explain? I've gotta get dressed. *(He exits.)*

SLOANE: Bran-don! *(To* DOUG*)* Hi. Hi. My name is Sloane. When I came over that day I didn't know about you and I was afraid Brandon may have said stuff about me and so, well—God this is embarrassing—I pretended to be this girl in my office, Liz. I went to Brearly with her and she's really nice.

DOUG: So you pretended to be this Liz chick? *(Pause)* That's awesome! I wanna do that, I'm totally gonna do that. "Yo, I'm Dwayne."

SLOANE: Sorry, I'm Sloane Hudson.

DOUG: Sloane. Oh. OH.

(Enter BRANDON.*)*

BRANDON: *(To* SLOANE*)* You guys all straight now?

DOUG: Yeah, she's Sloane, *Sloane of the Hudson.* I got it, no big whup. And I'm Roger Federface. *(Swings tennis racquet)* Ace!

BRANDON: Listen, I really gotta go. Sloane, you headed out? *(He heads for the door.)*

SLOANE: Nope, I've got something for Pogo.

BRANDON: You're staying?

SLOANE: If that's okay.

DOUG: Sure! She can wait with me for Tush!

BRANDON: *(Mad)* Oh, Jesus, Doug, I'm not getting into that.

SLOANE: *(To* BRANDON*)* Are you okay?

BRANDON: I'm just stressed that's all.

DOUG: Buffer's just pissed 'cause he thinks I did something really stupid *and* he doesn't want to sell his little buddies.

SLOANE: Little buddies?

DOUG: His sperms.

BRANDON: Can we not…

DOUG: *(To* SLOANE*)* Look, we've gotta know. Would you really put them in the freezer?

SLOANE: Would I…yeah, that's the plan.

DOUG: And you'd pay for them?

BRANDON: We are not talking about this.

DOUG: *(To* BRANDON*)* See dude, I told you, she's not kidding.

BRANDON: Look, I said we're not talking about this!

DOUG: Bro, I know, but the insurance fuck up has really fucked us up—

BRANDON: I will figure that out Doug! I'm figuring that out *now.*

DOUG: It's the insurance company dude, it's like Darth Vader, get real.

BRANDON: I've got it under control.

DOUG: But Buffer, listen, we'll sell The Nap— And anyway she may not use it, right Sloane? It may just sit there with the Ben and Jerry's forever, right? Sloane?

SLOANE: That's true. That's *true.* The Nap? What's that?

DOUG: Bro, it's like a great backup plan in case—

BRANDON: OH MY GOD DOUG!

SLOANE: What's The Nap?

DOUG: I mean, what's the downside bro? Besides being a Dad? You would be a great Dad.

SLOANE: I don't see the downside for you guys really.

DOUG: And I would be a great Uncle, like totally chill.

SLOANE: At this point it's really a win-win for everyone.

DOUG: See, Buff, it's a win-win.

SLOANE: *(To* DOUG*)* It's a win win! Go team!

SLOANE & DOUG: Go team, go team, go team, GO TEAM! Sperm Sperm Sperm Sperm!

BRANDON: OKAY! OKAY. Okay, I'm COMPLETELY against it, I must be insane, but SHIT HAPPENS. So fine, yes, I'll do it.

DOUG: All right! All right!

SLOANE: All right!

BRANDON: But Sloane, if I'm gonna you know, be your *donor*, we probably shouldn't go out anymore.

DOUG: Oh.

SLOANE: Oh.

BRANDON: I want to and all but it's really too complicated.

DOUG: Oh.

SLOANE: Oh, really.

BRANDON: Yes.

(Beat)

SLOANE: Okay, I mean it wasn't like a heavy thing, between us.

BRANDON: No, it was just fun.

SLOANE: Yeah, fun, we weren't even officially like *dating.*

(Pause)

BRANDON: This is so fucked.

(BRANDON *exits the apartment.*)

(*Pause*)

(SLOANE *bursts into tears.*)

SLOANE: I hate him. I *hate* him.

DOUG: But he's gonna do your deal!

(SLOANE *cries.* DOUG *looks around for something to give to her and grabs his pajama bottoms. She continues to cry and then realizes that she's crying into his pj's and gingerly puts them down.*)

SLOANE: I never cry. I never cry. When my parents got divorced I didn't cry. When I didn't get into Princeton I didn't cry. When I flunked Organic Chem I didn't cry. When I…when I… Ohhhhh. (*She really starts bawling.*)

DOUG: Hold on, I'm gonna get you a beer. (*He goes to the frig and gets a beer.*)

(SLOANE *cries some more.*)

(DOUG *brings her a beer.*)

DOUG: Here, you can cry in your beer now.

(DOUG *and* SLOANE *laugh.*)

SLOANE: You're crazy. TBI.

DOUG: TBI.

(DOUG *and* SLOANE *laugh harder.*)

DOUG: You dig the Buffman?

SLOANE: When I don't HATE him.

DOUG: I don't think he knows.

SLOANE: That's because he's stupid.

DOUG: He doesn't think you'd go for him, not really.

SLOANE: Boys are so stupid.

DOUG: Yeah, we are. But we're…cool.

SLOANE: But what did he mean that shit happened?

DOUG: Oh, a shitload of shit. There was big insurance screw up with our Mom and also…something's missing, Buffer thinks somebody stole it…I don't, but he's super pissed and it might be worth a lot of money.

SLOANE: What's missing? The Nap? What is the friggin Nap?

DOUG: Napoleon Lajoie, he's in the Hall of Fame, was a Triple Crown winner.

SLOANE: He's a horse?

DOUG: No, he's a second baseman! I have his *card*. The Nap.

SLOANE: I get it. How did you lose it?

DOUG: It's not lost! It's missing, there's a big difference! It's not lost!

SLOANE: Okay, okay, *missing*.

DOUG: I know where it is, I mean I know who has it, Tush…Katerina has it.

SLOANE: Why does she have it?

DOUG: She's gonna show it to her cousin who's like this dealer dude so he'll give us an estimate.

(DOUG *pulls out the Baba necklace and shows it to* SLOANE.)

DOUG: She gave me this, you know, to hold on to. Her Baba gave it to her.

SLOANE: (*Looking at the Baba necklace*) I see. So, what's Katerina's last name?

DOUG: Tushenko. I call her "Tush".

SLOANE: Katerina Tushenko. And where does she live?

DOUG: In Queens.

SLOANE: Does she work…like a real job?

DOUG: She's a hostess somewhere on Lex… It's just five, right?

SLOANE: It's closer to five thirty.

DOUG: Five-thirty? Oh, Lordy, Lordy, I'm feeling poorly.

SLOANE: Oh, no.

DOUG: I'm a piece of crap. I'm fucked, I fucking fucked up, I believed her—

SLOANE: No, you're not Doug, you're smart, you're funny…

DOUG: I'm an asshole—

SLOANE: Doug, you are not an asshole, don't say that—

DOUG: Yes I am, I am.

SLOANE: *(Trying to distract him)* Look what I brought for Pogo. Crickets, they're nice and small. *(Tries to show them to* DOUG*)* And they're good luck too you know.

DOUG: Right. Like I have any luck. How could I, I'm a total idiot.

SLOANE: C'mon Doug, that's not true at—

DOUG: I am! I jumped out a fucking window and almost killed myself, why? To impress a bunch of fucking assholes? I fucked up, I fucked everything up the way I always fuck up.

SLOANE: No, no, Doug, you didn't.

DOUG: I wrecked my whole life, and I keep wrecking it— *(He grabs the recycling that's in the living room, moves it to the kitchen and sets it down with a bang.)*

SLOANE: You didn't wreck your life. A terrible thing happened to you. Terrible things happen to people. A terrible thing happened to me too.

DOUG: No it didn't.

SLOANE: Yes it did. A really awful thing happened to me. At Cornell. *(Pause)* In the basement of AD, actually.

DOUG: The basement…of Alpha Delt.

SLOANE: I know, Alpha Delt. Weird, huh?

DOUG: What. What happened?

SLOANE: I woke up there. On the pong table. Isn't that a riot? I'm still laughing.

(Pause)

DOUG: Oh. That is so fucked, that is so not right. I feel so bad.

SLOANE: You had nothing to do with it Doug.

DOUG: But those were *my* guys. I should do something now.

SLOANE: They were not your guys.

DOUG: Look, if you want me to kill any of those creeps you just tell me, I mean it. Or do some ritual for bad luck? I know this dude from South Carolina whose mother knows all this white magic. I'm serious. That shit works.

SLOANE: I'm fine now, really. And it was hard, really hard, every day it's hard, but I don't live there anymore. I live here, now. And you should too. Okay?

DOUG: Okay.

SLOANE: Neither one of us is going back there anymore, that's over.

DOUG: We have today and tomorrow.

SLOANE: That's right. *(She notices the panties on the wall.)* And we're taking down these stupid panties. It's stupid.

DOUG: Sorry about that.

(SLOANE *takes the panties off the wall and drops them into the garbage.*)

(*She picks up the recycling in the kitchen and returns it to the living room. Then she picks up the tux and heads for the door.*)

DOUG: Hey, Sloane?

(SLOANE *stops and turns toward* DOUG.)

DOUG: I've never been to a fashion show.

(SLOANE *holds out her arm to* DOUG.)

(*Blackout*)

Scene Nine

(BRANDON'*s classroom.* DOUG *enters holding a medium size manila envelope.*)

DOUG: Yo, Buffman.

BRANDON: Bro. What are you doing here?

DOUG: (*Looking around*) This is so cool, smells like Cheerios. (*Sniffs*) Or the zoo.

BRANDON: Dude, is everything okay?

DOUG: (*Waving to the portraits of all the Presidents*) Hey guys, how's it hanging?

BRANDON: How'd you get in?

DOUG: I said I was your brother. Your twin brother. The twin part really threw them off.

BRANDON: But how'd you get here?

DOUG: I walked from work, Mush for Brains.

BRANDON: You walked. That's forty blocks. Did you get fired?

DOUG: You're so negative. Mr Kim loves me these days. I told him Tom Cruise was my cousin.

BRANDON: Tom Cruise?

DOUG: Well, he could be…like we're all related dude. Justin Beiber's related to Ben Franklin. I read it on Buzzfeed.

BRANDON: What's going on Doug? Why'd you come?

(DOUG *shows* BRANDON *the manila envelope:*)

DOUG: This came certified, for me. But like I'm too chicken to open it. Maybe it's that ticket I got in Tahoe, remember when I crashed the van?

BRANDON: Dude, that was years ago!

DOUG: I don't think I paid. There could be interest maybe.

BRANDON: Give it to me.

DOUG: Maybe we should just throw it away.

BRANDON: *(Holds his hand out)* No, give it to me.

DOUG: Maybe we should tear it up. *(He makes a tearing motion.)*

BRANDON: Doug, hand it over.

(DOUG *holds the envelope over his head, taunting* BRANDON.)

DOUG: Come and get it. Come and get it.

(DOUG *dances around the classroom. Thrusts the envelope in front of* BRANDON, *who grabs for it and misses.*)

BRANDON: Bro, I'm not in the mood for this.

DOUG: *(Teasing)* Maybe it's something good.

(DOUG *thrusts it in front of* BRANDON *again, who grabs it, but* DOUG *grabs it back.*)

BRANDON: DOUG! I'm not playing this game.

DOUG: Doug, I'm not playing this game.

BRANDON: Cut it out.

DOUG: Cut it out.

(BRANDON *lunges for* DOUG, *they wrestle, and* BRANDON *grabs the envelope. He sees that it's been opened.*)

BRANDON: What the hell is this Doug? You opened it! (*He reaches in and pulls out small envelope.*)

DOUG: Maybe.

(BRANDON *opens envelope and pulls out a note.*)

BRANDON: (*Reads note*) "I am sorry I miss the tennis."

DOUG: Tush! It's Tush!

BRANDON: "But I half to go to Tallinn. My mother in car crush. Sergei said ninety-two grand. Hope I come back. Keep Baba necklace safe. Love, Katerina" And, holy shit— (*He pulls out The Nap.*) What! Are you kidding? The Nap?

DOUG: I knew it, I knew there was a reason she didn't come!

BRANDON: (*Staring at The Nap*) I don't believe it! Infuckingincredible.

DOUG: And you ragged on Tush, Buffer, you were wrong man. *Wrong.*

BRANDON: Ninety-two grand…it must be autographed. Look, this must be it.

(BRANDON *and* DOUG *stare closely at the card.*)

DOUG: I thought that was just part of the card.

BRANDON: That must be an autograph. That's amazing.

DOUG: I am so glad that I didn't kill myself when I tried to kill myself just for *this moment*. This is one of the greatest moments ever.

BRANDON: It is bro, it is. Ninety two grand. Ninety two grand. Holy shit.

(BRANDON *and* DOUG *stare at the card some more.*)

DOUG: I told you she didn't steal it. I told you, I told Sloane— When you left she cried, she was so freaked out by you.

BRANDON: She cried?

DOUG: Yeah, she said she never cried, like ever--like not even when the thing happened at Cornell.

BRANDON: Sloane didn't go to Cornell she went to Dartmouth.

DOUG: She *started* at Cornell dude and transferred.

BRANDON: No, she didn't, she didn't tell me that.

DOUG: She left Cornell after…the thing…

BRANDON: What thing?

DOUG: You don't know?

BRANDON: I didn't even know she was *at* Cornell!

DOUG: Well, I can't tell you.

BRANDON: You gotta tell me now. What happened to her?

(Pause)

DOUG: A bad thing, in the AD basement. Like she woke up there. On the pong table. Idiot bros and such, do I need to spell it out for you?

BRANDON: Jesus. Jesus. Did she like…press charges?

DOUG: No, man, she just booked it outa there.

BRANDON: That's terrible, that's horrible. She never told me.

DOUG: Chicks always tell me stuff. She likes you, she told me.

BRANDON: What'd she say?

DOUG: She said she likes you. When she doesn't hate you.

BRANDON: See?

DOUG: No, dude, that's just girlspeak for she, you know, *loves* you.

BRANDON: C'mon…

DOUG: No, seriously, when they say hate they mean love. Like when they say they don't want to talk they mean they do, and when they say nothing's wrong they mean everything's wrong, don't you know this shit yet?

BRANDON: Did you figure all this out before or after you jumped out the window?

DOUG: I get women, dude, I was *born* getting women. I mean, people say women are all complicated and mysterious and stuff but they are simple, man. I mean there are some things that *all* women like—it doesn't matter how liberated and feminated they are. Like-jewelry, they are totally hard wired for shiny and sparkly. Or *glitter*, they are suckers for glitter. Like a great present would be glitter in all kinds of colors. I knew this girl—she put it in her lady garden—you know what I'm saying? and I had that shit on my dick for weeks. I couldn't get those babies off. And bro, this is something not many people know, this is like secret information. You know what girls *really* like, like anywhere, anytime? I mean this makes them so happy. Unbelievably happy. I've tried it, it always works. *(Pause)* Bubbles.

BRANDON: Bubbles?

DOUG: Yeah, bubbles. You go to the toy store and you buy those bubbles that come with a wand and you just blow some and they start laughing and thinking it's so cute. I'm telling you. Bubbles. All chicks like bubbles. They totally love you for it dude. Bubbles.

BRANDON: Bubbles, thanks bro. Done.

DOUG: You'll see. So go ahead, call Sloane, now you can call her.

BRANDON: So, you told her all about The Nap and Katerina…

DOUG: Sloane met her, when she was Liz!

BRANDON: Oh, yeah.

DOUG: Do it dude.

BRANDON: Maybe.

DOUG: Don't be a dumb shit! We've got The Nap, now you don't have to sell your little buddies to Sloane. You can just *date* her.

BRANDON: Maybe.

DOUG: You like her. The Nap is back, The Nap is back! *(Shows the Presidents The Nap)* Boys, The Nap is back!

(Blackout)

Scene Ten

(A few days later)

(Coney Island)

(We hear noises of a carnival and see the colored lights in the distance, and the sign for the THUNDERBOLT ticket booth where SLOANE *stands now.)*

(She is punching out a text, clearly she's punching the same number/icon on her phone. She's mad.)

*(*BRANDON *comes rushing in.)*

*(*SLOANE *stares daggers at him.)*

BRANDON: I am so so sorry.

SLOANE: You're like a half an hour late!

BRANDON: I texted you.

SLOANE: You're still late.

BRANDON: You could've texted back.

SLOANE: I did.

BRANDON: *(He holds up his phone)* Push pins, why? Why push pins? You're weird. Listen, the truth is, the train/

SLOANE: Oh, God, I hate it when people say *the truth is,* it always means they're gearing up to tell you some big lie, forget it, I don't want to know—

BRANDON: Sloane—

SLOANE: No, *no,* and if you think I'm gonna go on this Thunderbolt death ride thing you can forget that too. I never go on rollercoasters, never, like I would never wear those socks with *toes* in them. Like never.

BRANDON: I think I have some socks with toes in them.

SLOANE: I'm sure you do. I'm serious, I'm not going on this thing. No way.

BRANDON: Okay, okay. I just thought it was a good place to meet. Since you've never been here before.

SLOANE: I didn't even know it was in Brooklyn. I thought it was an island, Coney Island.

BRANDON: It's a peninsula.

SLOANE: Peninsula. Spoken like a true middle school teacher, that is such a middle school word/

BRANDON: C'mon, let's go to the beach, I won't make you go on The Thunderbolt Death Ride, I promise.

SLOANE: Peninsula. Peninsula.

BRANDON: Isn't it cool here?

SLOANE: *(Unenthusiastic)* Yeah.

BRANDON: Excuse me, have you ever been to an amusement park before?

SLOANE: I went to a water park when I was little once. It was horrible. I went on this ride, Moby Dip, and I threw up.

BRANDON: Moby Dip?

SLOANE: It's true. Moby Dip.

BRANDON: I wanna go there.

SLOANE: Water parks, a festival of e-coli.

BRANDON: *(Thinking he's funny)* An e-coli family reunion!

(SLOANE *doesn't think* BRANDON's *funny and stares at him. He shrugs, sheepish.)*

SLOANE: So, how's Doug?

BRANDON: He's good. Actually this weekend he has a date. It's this girl where he works, Jin-souk. She lives with her uncle who's super strict but Doug told him we were related to Tom Cruise. Jeez, he hasn't been on a date in years. I'm gonna be a nervous wreck.

SLOANE: Tom Cruise?

BRANDON: I have no idea.

SLOANE: Why don't you tail them?

BRANDON: Sounds like something you would do.

SLOANE: *(Ignoring him)* Well, anyway, I've been thinking and—

BRANDON: I've been thinking too—

SLOANE: —I've decided to table the donor idea for now. It's probably more complicated than I thought.

BRANDON: It is.

SLOANE: I hope you're not angry. I mean I feel bad, I'm not someone who backs out/

BRANDON: No, no, it's totally okay.

SLOANE: You know, there's just all kinds of stuff, you'd have to sign a release, there are underlying nuances that are murky, you know--I'm sorry but/

BRANDON: It's fine, it's fine, I was having second thoughts too.

SLOANE: You were?

BRANDON: Yeah, I don't think I could have done it.

SLOANE: Great. I mean, not great but you know. Ah. So, how's Pogo?

BRANDON: Good. Kind and understanding. But tough, like you.

SLOANE: Tough like me?

BRANDON: In a good way. Clearly, you can handle the-- curve balls.

SLOANE: This must be serious, you're using sports analogies.

BRANDON: You know—life's unexpected challenges.

SLOANE: *(Surprised)* Doug talked to you.

BRANDON: He thought I knew.

SLOANE: He told you what happened.

BRANDON: I didn't know you were at Cornell.

SLOANE: Just Freshman year. I wish he hadn't said anything.

BRANDON: Why? Were you ever gonna tell me? *(Silence)* Well, were you?

SLOANE: I don't know Brandon, I wasn't sure I was ever gonna *see* you again.

BRANDON: I want to know all about you—

SLOANE: Stop. *(She looks away.)*

BRANDON: Hey, I have a surprise.

SLOANE: I hate surprises.

BRANDON: Close your eyes. Just do it. No cheating.

SLOANE: You're so bossy.

(SLOANE *closes her eyes and* BRANDON *reaches into his pocket, pulls out a bottle of bubbles, opens it and blows bubbles through the wand.)*

BRANDON: Open them.

(SLOANE *opens her eyes and is surrounded by a cloud of bubbles. She's alarmed.)*

SLOANE: Oh. God. *(She swats at the bubbles.)*

BRANDON: Don't you love them? *(He keeps making bubbles.)*

SLOANE: Brandon! This is so embarrassing, put them away! People are looking. And smiling at us. Gross.

BRANDON: I thought you would love them.

SLOANE: Really? Me? Bubbles?

BRANDON: It's like a universal thing.

SLOANE: Did you read that somewhere?

BRANDON: *(Putting the bubbles away)* More for me.

(Pause)

(BRANDON *pulls The Nap from his jacket pocket and shows it to* SLOANE.)

SLOANE: The Nap?? How'd you get it?

BRANDON: Katerina mailed it back, with a letter.

SLOANE: No way.

BRANDON: Look.

(BRANDON *shows* SLOANE *the letter.*)

BRANDON: Read it.

SLOANE: *(Reading letter)* Car *crush*, I love that. Car crush!

BRANDON: Amazing, huh?

SLOANE: Shocking. But people can surprise you…their better nature can win out.

BRANDON: *(Reading from letter)* Car *crush*, that's really funny. Super funny.

SLOANE: It is. She was very funny.

(Beat)

BRANDON: I just hope that nobody died.

SLOANE: What?

BRANDON: Or that you're not on some hit list now. You don't need a bodyguard, do you?

SLOANE: Brandon, seriously, I have absolutely no idea what you are talking about! Obviously Katerina felt bad and sent back The Nap.

(BRANDON *moves closer to* SLOANE.)

SLOANE: What are you doing?

BRANDON: I want to be closer to you. *(Does a Woody Allen impression)* "I have some very private, personal things to say to you about your emotional spectrum, and Dostoyevsky, and Fellini and…uh…playing the clarinet!"

SLOANE: *(Smiling)* You really annoy me.

BRANDON: And how's that love is just hormones thing going for you?

SLOANE: Good. Good.

BRANDON: And love's a fiction?

SLOANE: I like fiction. You know, good fiction.

BRANDON: I missed you.

SLOANE: No you didn't.

BRANDON: I did.

SLOANE: You're full of it.

BRANDON: I seriously missed you.

SLOANE: Right. What did you miss?

BRANDON: Well/

SLOANE: Maybe my jokes, you missed my jokes.

BRANDON: No, I didn't miss your jokes. I think…your chin. I missed your chin.

(SLOANE *is silent.*)

BRANDON: Did you miss me?

SLOANE: *(Lying)* No.

BRANDON: Maybe a little?

SLOANE: Not even a tad. *Tad.*

BRANDON: You did. You missed me.

SLOANE: Pe-nin-sula. I really like that word.

(Pause)

BRANDON: If we start now, you can still wear a bikini.

SLOANE: *(Sincere)* What!?

BRANDON: But my genes aren't perfect.

(BRANDON *and* SLOANE *move closer to each other.*)

SLOANE: Who's perfect?

BRANDON: Drinking…brothers who jump out windows…

(BRANDON *bumps* SLOANE *with his hip and she bumps back.*)

SLOANE: I know, but I don't care. I don't care.

(BRANDON *and* SLOANE *look at each other.*)

BRANDON: Sloane, did you get Katerina to return The Nap? Did you buy it back from her?

SLOANE: No. No. (*Smiling broadly*) NO.

(BRANDON *and* SLOANE *kiss.*)

(*They break away from the kiss and look at each other.*)

SLOANE: No.

(BRANDON *and* SLOANE *kiss again, a really good kiss.*)

(*The sound of the roller coaster whooshes by.*)

END OF PLAY

www.ingramcontent.com/pod-product-compliance
Lightning Source LLC
Chambersburg PA
CBHW061624130726
47996CB00003B/1121